WONDER

&

WRATH

A. M. Juster

PAUL DRY BOOKS

Philadelphia   *2020*

First Paul Dry Books Edition, 2020

Paul Dry Books, Inc.
Philadelphia, Pennsylvania
www.pauldrybooks.com

Printed in the United States of America

Library of Congress Control Number: 2020942393

For my wife Laura
and our children James and Caitlin,
who have all been good sports
about occasionally showing up in my poems

CONTENTS

INNER

OTHER

ACKNOWLEDGEMENTS

Alabama Literary Review "Completed Fragments of Rilke"; *America* "November Requiem"; *Angle* "Cassandra"; *Arion* "On the Death of a Most Honorable Man, Roger Manwood, Lord Chief Baron of the Queen's Exchequer"; *Barefoot Muse* "First Death"; *Better Than Starbucks* "Falling for the Witch"; *Café Review* "What Is Chosen in Dreams"; *Disclaimer* "Epilogue" "Escaping Myself" "Threat Levels"; *Evansville Review* "Autumn Night" "Three Visitors"; *First Things* "An Apostle Falls" "Farewell, Mr. Wizard" "Japanese Maple in January" "No Man's Island" "The Devil In the Details"; *The Formalist* "Rimbaud in Abyssinia" "Untamed Daughter"; *Hopkins Review* "Surveillance"; *Hudson Review* "Cuttyhunk, Late Afternoon"; *Magma* "I Sit Half-Naked"; *Measure* "Fruit Flies" "No" "The Minx"; *Measure Review* "Sundowning"; *National Review* "Behold" "Inertia"; *The New Criterion* "To My Dear Friend, M.J. Jackson, A Disparager of This Treatise"; *North American Review* "Rounding Up the Mimes"; *On the Seawall* "The impossible in which I believe"; *Orange Blossom Review* "Animal Model"; *Poetry* "East African Proverbs"; *Queen Mob's Tea House* "Sudden Onset"; *Rattle* "Heirloom" "To Her Husband for Beating Her" "Triptych: Dream, Convenience Store, Bar"; *Rosebud* "Visitation"; *Southwest Review* "A Kay Ryan Fanboy Poem" "A Midsummer Night's Hangover" "Autoimmune Attack"; *The Weekly Standard* "Scandinavian Homesick Blues"

The four Aldhelm riddles and "Eucheria's Impossibilities" appeared in *Saint Aldhelm's Riddles* (University of Toronto Press, 2015). "Eucheria's Impossibilities" also appeared in "A Brief and Inadequate History of Female Comic Poets" in the Summer/Fall 2014 issue of *Light*.

"Proposed Clichés" appeared in *Sleaze & Slander: New and Selected Comic Verse 1995–2015* (Measure Press, 2016).

"Crowded Skies" appeared in *The Billy Collins Experience* (Kelsay Books, 2016).

"No" won the 2006 Howard Nemerov Sonnet Award. "Fruit Flies" "Rimbaud in Abyssinia" and "Untamed Daughter" were finalists for the same award in other years.

"November Requiem" was one of three runner-ups for the 2014 Foley Poetry Award sponsored by *America*.

I am grateful to Aaron Poochigian for his advice on the Housman and Aldhelm translations, to Clive Watkins and Laura Mali-Astrue for their advice on the Rimbaud translation, and to Eurig Salisbury for his advice on the Mechain translation.

WONDER

&

WRATH

OUTER

Heirloom

I know that I was suckered in:
firm curves bulging, olive skin,
perfectly well-rounded cheeks
rubified with port-wine streaks,
the saffron crown with one deep crack,
an eggplant-colored nob in back—
a touch of tumor. It would still
be sunning on my windowsill—
art illustrating daily life—
except I took my carving knife
and slowly sliced five slabs of fresh,
soil-sweet, yet vaguely bitter flesh.

Animal Model

From sunless humming basement rooms there comes
that stench of urine-drenched wood chips and shit
in cages piled up to the ceiling tiles.

Small grafted tumors bloom from pale shaved skin.
Some mice don't rest; they test their bars for hours
as others lie alone until they die.

For nervous breakdown, lab technicians make
a food dispenser—like our straw dispensers.
Rats quickly learn a tap will earn a pellet.

They press down ever faster on the lever,
then take a break to gorge and grip their food
like misers holding unexpected gold.

Chins sag and haunches spread; energy lags.
When pressing on the lever seems obsessive,
a post-doc tells the techs to stop the pellets.

Soon rats are banging harder on that bar;
they keep at it until exhaustion kills
their frenzy, then they droop into a stupor.

The techs inject the rodents with new compounds.
Within a week or so the cohort will
be "sacrificed" and challenged neurons sliced.

My neurons fray the way theirs do—when boards
politely loot, or parents brutalize,
or friends will never wake to hear farewell.

I Sit Half-Naked

with my socks still on, my gown half-open
because this teaching hospital believes
that dignity disrupts efficiency,
and all there is for anyone to read
is one brochure in Spanish: EL DOLOR,
which after thirty-seven minutes gets
my full attention, then, before long, gains
my full approval as I dwell upon
what doctors call "depression" and the way
that term suggests a highway's dip and rise,
not the last lonely exit on a road
to nowhere growing narrower and dark
until you stop, besieged by underbrush,
then I remember how economists
contend that a recession's depth portends
the strength of the recovery to come,
thus a depression should be followed by
a geyser of exuberant new goods
(which is a promise mostly left unkept),
and, finally, how tropical depressions
pummel shores, then shortly later grace
unblemished sky with unexpected azure,
but Spanish, it abhors our metaphor,
so *el dolor*—a sadness with no bounds
or schedule, only unspecific loss,
describes a world of closed, dead circuitry
that leaves us mourning those we lose to grief.

The door snaps open and I hear him say,
"Sorry I'm late. So how are we today?"

Behold

Let the state highway cleave cold, stubbled fields
so that both empty lanes extend like grace,
and let prim churches in the ratio
of seven Baptist to each Methodist
appear with rigid regularity
close to the road, their dead even closer
with small, flat rusting markers on most graves,
then drive another twenty minutes more
to see the trees defer to furrowed soil
except for this one rise where pines aspire
to reach where crows and turkey vultures rule,
and let those who have nursed the dirt behold
the blush and burgundies of morning clouds
that do not stifle early rays of sun
from blanketing the hillside's eastern slope
where mothers, fathers, aunts and uncles wait
and gravestones chalice that unearthly light.

A. M. JUSTER

Threat Levels

The level yesterday was red,
the color on the splattered dead.

The level for today is green,
although the chatter stays obscene.

Tomorrow's level will be gray
as light is lost throughout the day.

Epilogue

The caution tape is tattered
and flapping in the wind.
Birds guard the median
where glass and steel lie shattered.

There are no robins hymning
or gawkers at this scene—
only a lowered sun,
raw cries of crows, and dimming.

Farewell, Mr. Wizard

I conjure NBC in black-and-white.
You drop dry ice in water; fog is rising.
You sell us Celsius and Fahrenheit.

I lose you in a cloud of advertising—
Winston, Esso, Zenith, Mr. Clean,
those thirty second breaks for Ovaltine—
then smile at Bunsen burners and balloons,
more ropes and pulleys. You are mesmerizing
as familiar things become surprising.
I dream of robots, rayguns, Mars and moons,
and know for sure our Chevrolet will fly.

POOF! *Static.* I can't make your show go on.
Space shuttles fall; the pumps are running dry.
Jihadists shop for warheads. Godspeed, Don.

Cassandra

We kissed; he spat. Apollo's spite results
in visions that dissolve the future's veils
so stonework runs like water, time reveals
that chance is fraud, and prophecies turn false.
He knows I see Troy's butchered men convulse
beside dry corpses as his brilliance pales
on western waves. He suffers no appeals
no matter how I suffer for his faults.

Lush memories decay before my eyes.
I sense which virgin will be raped today,
which nation crumbles. My beheading is
still years ahead. I cannot pray to die
nor alter blood revenge that I foresee;
a blade is always being honed for me.

Falling for the Witch

He did not hear our warnings. In his world,
his heady world of rapture and surprise,
what she demanded promised ecstasy.
He thought that others did not understand.

His heady world of rapture and surprise
sustained delusion. When he dreamed of her,
he thought that others did not understand,
although her grasp grew stronger. Over time

sustained delusion when he dreamed of her
was stripping him of everything divine.
Although her grasp grew stronger over time,
he did not sense her fingers on his throat.

Was stripping him of everything divine
what she demanded? Promised ecstasy,
he did not sense her fingers on his throat;
he did not hear our warnings in his world.

Inertia

High glinting leaves,
glazed by the post-storm light,
are hushing dusk
in reassuring waves.

Our lichen-clad
old maple lost three limbs
to rain that felt
like reprimands from God.

Scraggly, and cut
unevenly for years
to spare town wires,
it angles toward the street.

When summer cedes
to autumn's middle age
of rust and squash,
the threat to neighbors fades,

so we will wait,
though soon the driven ice
will trap its wood
in gleaming, fatal weight.

Surveillance

Jackbooted jays,
the two who try
to eat small eggs
nestled in holly,
return to eye
our sparrows' young.
In glittering,
corrosive sun,
they seem to savor
how their prey
keeps quavering
and squittering.

They dive and veer,
and rise to rest
on splintered pickets,
then brashly fly
through walls of leaves.
It's obvious
what they will do—
the coming days
shall see a flash
in azure sky
of ravenous
and jagged blue.

Vertigo

The world turns liquid, reels and rolls,
     as gravity

veers at angles; what was still
     is blurred and whirled.

Revolutions echo; you lie
     still for hours,

too weak for vomiting and still
     too dazed for prayer.

No whiz-bang device can repair
     your inner ear;

doctors try shifting crystal shards,
     like sad wizards.

Sometimes it's magic, sometimes not—
     they never know.

They never know what to advise
     if that trick fails.

Focus your eyes on horizons,
     one whispered once.

It helps to refocus the brain;
     the brain resets.

The brain can reset in the ways
     my father's did.

When his tumor nicked a vein,
     cells drowned in blood.

His bloodied brain regathered words,
      word word by word.

Grace is not crystalline, but grit
      that squints at pain.

Grace is the will to retake things,
      thing thing by thing.

No Man's Island

for JFK, Jr.

A strip of violet quivers in the haze—
a near-mirage above the furrowed grays
and blues of Vineyard Sound, an afterthought
of wind-worn scrub the military bought
and then abandoned.
                  Peace returned except
for sea that pummels shoreline. Surf has swept
away most tools of combat, though in dense
tangles of grass and vines old armaments
remain as lattices of rusted lace.

Signs tell the curious to leave this place,
but squadrons of resurgent birds ignore
these teetering commands of the Cold War;
gulls bomb the rocks with crabs. A few miles north,
two shrouded boats are crossing back and forth
as if to mark where Camelot's last son
thought he could see the sky where there was none.

Cuttyhunk, Late Afternoon

Small white terns are swarming in a dense cloud
that convulses through new forms as it arcs
and ascends, then veers and grazes the sea.

A thin violet slash is writhing with fish
that are feeding on the shelf right off shore;
the cloud rains down hard again and again.

In the teeming frenzy over the chop,
flecks of silver gleam, unfathomably,
but the prey do not abandon their space.

After eighteen minutes, violet succumbs
to rich blue. Abruptly, hundreds of birds
in formation race one island away.

November Requiem

Wood sways and mutters; palsied shutters bang.
The call has come. Stripped of starlight, night
dwindles to gritty lavender and gray;
mad jags of wind keep drowning out the surf.
We dress, then slog through beach plums to the bay.

Three days before, we calmed three bottlenoses
then led an exodus into the channel
to confront the bellowing Atlantic.
We roared, and told *Eyewitness News* that "tides
or virus-damaged ears" had made them frantic.

Now we return; salvation did not last.
Just yards from shore, they do not move at all
except to veer away as we draw near,
their faith in our benevolence betrayed
and their desire for surrender clear.

Three Visitors

Mist on moonspill   as midnight nears.
Adrift but not dreaming   our drowsy son
is covered and kissed.   At the kitchen door
our old basset is barking;   coyotes out back
are standing like statues   down by the dogwoods.
Across the crystal   of crusted snow,
they search for stragglers   to startle and chase.
Their vigil reveals   no victims this night.

Trash would be trouble;   they trot away
unbothered by bloodthroated   growling and baying.
No star distracts   their stealthy march.
As the highway hums   they howl through the calm,
then savor new scents   that spice their path
in this world awash   in wonder and wrath.

The Devil in the Details

Slow, old python of my Everglades,
he astutely picks where he invades:
data dumps; the depths of lower courts;
knotted weeds in annual reports.

Rounded figures fail to square; a will
screws the worthy with a codicil.
Minds don't meet as handshake deals unravel.
Lawyered butchers walk; accountants cavil.

Hear him honing clauses. Hear his hiss
polish premises and promises.
Check where he has brushed.
                              Sly visits leave
parasites no handlers perceive:
propositions snaking through the skin
set to spawn in pustules of fresh sin.

Autoimmune Attack

Far reaches of my realm are livid now—
more like inflamed. I missed the early signs
of weakness: slow corrosion in the walls;
corrupted arteries, and mute contempt
for arms of centralized authority.
New carnage comes without a warning shot
as traitors slide past lines of my defenses.
Appeals for calm embolden sleeper cells;
cascades of new betrayals take their toll.

I cannot crack the code. What makes them choose
an insurrection pairing suicide
with slaughter? Isn't there some formula
for peace? Perhaps a frank exchange of views?

Reports pile higher. I ignore the news.

Rounding Up the Mimes

They shunned the suburbs, trailer parks and farms.
Somewhere they had their silent neighborhood—
for who has ever lived next door to mimes?

Wherever they did live, they paid their taxes
from pocket change, obeyed our traffic laws,
and turned their radios down very low
so passers-by would never hear their songs.

Lacking identifiable positions
on anything important, they seemed . . . "Swiss."
White face paint hinted at a racist past.
When tabloids called, they never would deny
connections with the Mafia or Roswell.
At the French Embassy, a mime was hung
by his suspenders as a mob denounced
Marcel Marceau; some vigilantes smeared
a mime with bacon fat and chicken feathers,
then left him flailing by a KFC;
kids trapped another inside a box
of glass for days—and told him to "pretend
to eat a sandwich." For their own protection,
all mimes were taken into custody.

We watched as they were crowded into vans,
still gesturing with pouts and outstretched palms.

A. M. JUSTER

INNER

The impossible in which I believe

Borges is in; this library
is more alive. When he arrives,
the possible becomes more so.

I offer him his cup of tea,
but it is seldom tea-time where
Borges is. In this library

the volumes ripple on the shelves
and yet are rising like the fire
the possible becomes. More so

than you might think, these books extend
through time or space when it is clear
Borges is in. This library

is never ghostless as it glows
through dreams of visitors who know
the possible becomes more, so

much more than those who graced these aisles,
than dust that dances over files.
Borges is in this library;
the possible becomes more so.

Kennings

The Canada goose   came at the Mexican,
came at him hard   flapping and hissing,
its long outlandish   elastic neck
coiling and uncoiling   as it strained to strike.
When he could speak   he spat these words:

COBRA CHICKEN!   ***COBRA CHICKEN!***

—more proof of the point   that Norman nobles
laid waste to the land   but left us kennings,
those meldings of nouns   that name the unknown
to tame the unknown   as we do with death:

sword-sleep for Saxons   **dirt-nap** today.

They refashioned fear   of the infinite ocean
by paving a whale-road,   a track to be traveled
by mounting a sea-steed.   Dreams dwindle
as nightmares change;   your children may need:

drone-heart death-lackey   home-skulker hate-vessel

An Apostle Falls

Betrayal had fulfilled the prophecy.
Too proud for penance and too weak to run,
he strung himself up from a cedar tree
and swayed for days beneath a scathing sun.

Thieves cut his desiccated body free,
then left it in the dust. Throughout that night,
Jerusalem kept shuddering with light.

Japanese Maple in January

All spring she brushed aside my arguments
it would be cheaper, and would make more sense,
to fill the yard with hardy native stock.
She bought her maple, junked the chain-link fence,
and tried to start a lawn; our crabby flock
of grackles grew too fat on seed to quarrel.
While masons tamed the mud with slate and rock,
she planted birches, hollies and a laurel.
New pickets kept our neighbors in their place.

October stripped her birches down to bone,
as if to warn the weak. Beside new stone
the pygmy flares with plum and amber lace.
As ice storms make old oaks bow, crack and groan,
her gift keeps shimmering with fragile grace.

Visitation

We wander at the scene
of first and final love,
and what was there remains:

warm light through window panes,
a call across the courtyard,
the bristling of elms
with offhand majesty.

Untamed Daughter

. . . come, Kate, come, you must not look so sour.
—The Taming of the Shrew

At fourteen she loves being critical
and tells me, "Shakespeare uses language well,
but could have been, like, more original . . ."
I sputter, but rebuttals fail to jell.
All those recycled plots make it appear
to her he was a sneaky plagiarist—
no better than that girl expelled last year—
so "they" should take him off her reading list.

Please, Caitlin, let it go; great writers borrow
like gamblers. Don't begrudge the Bard a source
that he reshaped into Verona's sorrow,
Miranda's tenderness or Lear's remorse,
but mark him down a point or two
because he tamed a Kate as fierce as you.

A Midsummer Night's Hangover

Bottom finds novel uses for his ears
and muzzle, thus persuading everyone
he is, indeed, an ass. Titania slips
away with Oberon, and somehow lust
erupts in ways that were unseen on stage.
Beer flows, and fairies dance until the dawn.

The players wake to a diminished world
and mourn the lost bewitchment of their night.
Light pummels their defense of lidded eyes,
and parents speak in painful decibels.
To add more anguish, Mr. Henderson
had said that they must strike the set by noon.

Dyspeptic Puck yanks birches from their stands;
mechanicals unhook the fruitless moon.
Demetrius considers Helena
in jeans, and mopes as he recalls her strands
of spotlit hair. Fair Hermia still beams—
and reaches for Lysander in her dreams.

Fruit Flies

They are the best, as pest invasions go:
no bites and no disease, just clouds of small
tan smudges spawned in week-old grapes. Though slow,
they flit and frustrate like a knuckleball.
You kill a few, but not enough. You curse
as they outsmart you with their tiny brains;
bug spray could hurt you worse than them. What's worse,
you know that they keep breeding in your drains.

Pour some white wine into a dish, and wait.
They sense the sweetness, then the alcohol.
They cluster on the rim and hesitate,
but soon cannot resist your Riesling's call.
They soak in joy, relax, then drink no more.
It's no surprise—you've seen it all before.

A. M. JUSTER

First Death

You join, design a lifelike avatar,
complete a form that tells them who you are,
then download from your buddy list. You wait.
They never drop a hint about your fate,
so you must monitor your cyberclone,
which checks out websites, gossips on the phone,
and looks for singles in the neighborhood;
it's programmed to behave the way you would.
Weeks—maybe years—may pass, then some physician
calmly diagnoses your condition,
drunk accountants cream your minivan,
or you are wounded by an unknown man;
it doesn't matter. Friends are notified
that it is time to hustle to your side.
Some visit; others just refuse to go
without clear reasons why. You never know.
You write a will and pick a charity,
and see mistakes with blinding clarity.
You're told heroic measures are in vain
as vital signs decay. You pray the pain
will go away, although it never will.
Your cyberimage shudders, then it's still.
For the obituary, they create
the text, but no one cares that it's untrue.
You have no password, nothing you can do.
Decomposition? Usually dull.
Suits fray and features shrivel on the skull.
They have a coffin light you can adjust.
Wait long enough, bones crumble into dust.

Sudden Onset

They stay upbeat, then say,
"What doesn't kill you makes you stronger"—
that classic Nietzschean cliché.

We'll know before much longer.

The problem is it's true
for hate and tumors too.

A. M. JUSTER

After Scattering
David Berman's Ashes

Worker of words   maker of meter
lover of lines   and mercy in law

Reconciler   of rhythms and rules
defender of faith   doubter of God

Wanderer once   in a riven South
Brahmin by will   not birth or wealth

Friend and counselor   a force in court
champion of clarity   classics and charity

late in life   a braver of love
a father adopted   by daughters and sons

Apologizer   for politics and puns
eye-twinkler   near wine or wit

Scavenger of insight   in poetry and prose
heart that would rise   when an aria rose

Triptych: Dream,
Convenience Store, Bar

I

A vial, a syringe, a long thin flow
of hope is rising. Desperate to know
fatigue and chemofog will dissipate.
The dead have called, but vaguely wait.

II

KENTS. Gum. *The Globe*. No milk has sold for days.
He asks the clerk how much the jackpot pays.
Frayed wallet; photo of a woman buried
long ago nearby. They never married.

III

Two smiles. One wink. The usual appears
although she hasn't been here for years.
She cracks a joke about her latest breakup.
Reflection. Mother's grimace through the makeup.

Sundowning

We flip on every light again at eight;
that flimsy gambit fails at one a.m.
Dread varnishes her eyes. She paces, whines,
then starts to coil. We grab the leash and jackets.

In Druid moonlight, crickets—thinned by crows
and frost—replay low chords. A possum silvers
through pachysandra; sleek suburban cats
are prowling as if dinner is in doubt.

We plod in numb, arthritic steps, uphill
at first to make returning easier.
Back home exhaustion tolerates gray sleep,
the Judas kiss of this indifferent world.

No

No, not this time. I cannot celebrate
a man's discarded life, and will not try;
these knee-jerk elegies perpetrate
Plath's nightshade lies. Why should we glorify
descent into a solipsistic hell?
Stop. Softly curse the waste. Don't elevate
his suffering to genius. Never tell
me he will live on. Never call it fate.

Attend the service. Mourn. Pray. Comfort those
he lacerated. Keep him in your heart,
but use that grief to teach. When you compose
a line, it is a message, not just art.
Be furious with me, but I refuse
to praise him. No, we have too much to lose.

A. M. JUSTER

A Kay Ryan Fanboy Poem

At first
few of us see
the wry in her verse
the zen or the why.
No glance
lingers
long enough
to trust dips and slants
that wring the world
for a chance at truth.
Hocus-pocus like hers
is rarely discussed
even as blurs
come into focus.
Neurons adjust.

Rimbaud in Abyssinia

Teeth in a hyena's face/always slide into place
—Oromo proverb

Harar. Like syphilitic sores, time runs
down to crust. Vultures dawdle in the haze.
Between seasons for trading slaves or guns,
he doctors his accounts. It takes him days
to capture everything: one zebra skin,
twelve Remingtons and fifty rosaries,
receipts, expenses, fluctuations in
exchange rates, livestock, men lost to disease.

The Paris literati track down trails
of sex and words he mocks as juvenile.
Fearful of Muslim blades and Belgian jails,
he stashes fawning letters in a file
behind thick folders documenting sales.
Alone, he flashes that hyena smile.

Proposed Clichés

Softer than an old potato
too moldy to mash.

More user-friendly than a hooker
hard up for cash.

Love is like a hard-time sentence—
but better than cancer.

Ask not what your country can do,
for fear of the answer.

Beauty beheld is merely skin-deep;
infections are deeper.

The price of honesty is steep;
candidates are cheaper.

A drowning man may clutch at straws,
but his sipping is pathetic.

Burn the candle at both ends
if you want to wax poetic.

You can call off your dogs,
but your cats will ignore you.

If actuaries had wings,
they still would just bore you.

An apple a day keeps the doctor away,
but not your disease.

Blood is thicker than water,
except when they freeze.

It's just spilt milk under the bridge,
so don't be big babies.

If you're crazy like a fox,
get tested for rabies.

OTHER

East African Proverbs

Let the relentless fist
be kissed.

The salt cannot be cooked;
the past is overlooked.

Full once they nibble,
fleas quibble.

Teeth in a hyena's face
always slide into place.

No donkey can cart
what weighs down your heart.

Outside a man is respected;
at home that man is neglected.

The strangers weep and leave;
family members grieve.

Even half-blind men
hope to see again.

True words end;
lies extend.

(Translated from Oromo)

The Minx

In the paneled dining room, imbued
With fruit and varnish, I, without a care,
Pick a plate of dicey Belgian food
And amuse myself in my huge chair.

Glad and shy while I'm eating, time ticks by.
Kitchen doors blow open with a gust
—Then this servant blows in (I don't know why),
Kerchief loose, hairdo coyly mussed.

And while her quaking pinkie slides down
Her pale orange-pink cheek with velvet down
As she's pouting like a three-year-old,

Tight in to lull me, she sets plates out
—Then, like *that* (to get a kiss, no doubt)
Whispers, "Feel right here; my cheek is cold . . ."

(Translated from the French of Rimbaud)

　　　A. M. JUSTER

To Her Husband for Beating Her

Through your heart's lining let there be pressed—slanting down—
  A dagger to the bone in your chest.
  Your knee crushed, your hand smashed, may the rest
  Be gutted by the sword you possessed.

(Translated from the Middle Welsh of Gwerful Mechain)

Completed Fragments of Rilke

"Les Dieux: ces obstinés qui vivent . . ."

> *The Gods: recalcitrants who live*
> *in contradictions*, frauds who lie
> about which sins they must forgive,
> which joys they must deny.

"Quelle étrange passion . . ."

> *What peculiar passion*
> *transforms this large number*
> *of things as they slumber*
> *into words that fashion*
>
> *a silence of flowers*
> with roots that do not tire
> but bequeath desire
> in still perfect hours.

"Est-ce des Dieux en fuite . . ."

> *Is it the Gods in flight*
> *who make the sun resound*
> or is it human sight
> where glory can be found?

(Rilke's French is italicized)

Impossibilities

I'm longing for my golden metal threads that shine
    and bristly knotted hair to intertwine.

I chat about a gemstone-studded silken coat
    as if it were a garment made of goat.

A prince's purple and a homely rag are wed;
    a brilliant gem is fused with heavy lead.

Now let the pearl be robbed of glittering appeal
    and may it glow inside some gloomy steel.

Let emeralds be guarded with my Gallic brass;
    may sapphires now equal stones in class.

The jaspers, cliffs and boulders are the same, it's said.
    The moon now chooses darkness of the dead.

Let us tend lilies now where bramble grows;
    may dreaded hemlock clutch the crimson rose.

So, piling on, let us now wish for garbage fish
    while passing up a tasty seafood dish.

Let a toad love a bream, a bass his serpent too;
    may trout and snail pursue a rendezvous.

Let a low fox and highborn lioness romance;
    may a chimp give that pretty lynx a chance.

Let buck and donkey, tigress and wild ass now date;
    may nimble deer and sluggish cattle mate.

Now let a bitter herb befoul the sweet rose wine;
    may honey and repulsive gall combine.

Let's blend a canyon's crystal water with the mud;
      may our refreshing fountain stir up crud.

Let ghastly buzzards and swift swallows have their fling;
      may nightingales and dour owls now sing.

Let a stern screech-owl and his flashy partridge nest;
      may ravens and sweet doves embrace at rest.

Let creatures trade their turf for risky area
      as hicks and slaves pursue Eucheria.

(Translated from the sixth/seventh century Latin of Eucheria)

A. M. JUSTER

Riddles from
Saint Aldhelm's *Aenigmata*

6

I share now with the surf one destiny
In rolling cycles as each month repeats.
As beauty in my brilliant form retreats,
So too the surges fade in cresting sea.

21

With flesh that's furrowed and a bluish glow,
I'm formed to grind crude metal with each row.
Smoothing gold hoards and ore is what I know.
Remaining coarse, I keep a surface sleek;
While lacking speech, I croak a raucous shriek.

23

Twin sisters, Nature once produced us two
Controlled by laws considered always true.
We hate complainers and to law we hew.
For mortals of our age joy would ensue,
If they could heed the standard sisters do.

49

As pounded, gaping metal—wide, gross, round—
I hang untouched by sky or boundless ground.
Glowing in flames and fevering with bubbles,
I thus confront two fronts with different troubles
As I survive both being scorched and drowned.

(Translated from the Latin; answers are on page 75)

On the Death of a Most Honorable Man, Roger Manwood, Lord Chief Baron of the Queen's Exchequer

The burglar's nightmare, somber scourge of rakes,
Jove's Hercules, a vulture to a thug,
Lies in an urn. Rejoice, you sons of crime.
Mourn, guiltless one, neck bowed with tangled hair;
The court's bright light, the pride of precedent,
Has died. Alas, great virtue fled with him
To Acheron's worn shores. For all his virtues,
Show mercy, spiteful man; don't be too brazen
With ash of one whose glances awed the mobs,
And so as Pluto's bloodless messenger
Assaults you, may bones find their joyous rest
And fame outlast a marble tomb's inscriptions.

(Translated from the Latin of Christopher Marlowe)

To My Dear Friend, M.J. Jackson,
A Disparager of This Treatise

In quiet, lonely country, roaming open fields,
    We both would watch the constellations play
Their light on vaults of frigid night as stars appeared
    Throughout the quenching of the fading day.
We watched. This poet, long before our light,
    Would watch it set upon the Romans' sea
And, ever mindful Mother Earth had made him mortal,
    Supplied us timeless stars in poetry
To give clear warning to the people yet to come
    So no one had to trust the deities.
These holy songs of Heaven that embrace the cosmos
    Were then inflicted with indignities,
And though their wreckage end up upon our shores,
    Their authorship was narrowly retained.
I couldn't bear to beg eternal gods, or stars
    Afflicting mortals with the preordained,
But, touched by love of virtue that will quickly pass,
    I searched for someone with determination;
A man, I chose a man, a brief and fleeting friend
    Who in my book should want this dedication.
O you who thrive or fall, I'd say, within these pages,
    Though with a name that merits living on:
I send this gift conveyed from western shores to you
    Who followed stars ascending at the dawn.
Come now, accept: that day we join the dead is coming,
    Which gives the dirt our bones as they decay
With spirits destined not to live eternally
    And bonds between dear friends that fade away.

(Translated from the Latin of A.E. Housman)

Escaping Myself

Absorbed by wine, I do not notice dusk.
The blossoms fill my clothing when they fall.

I stand up drunk, then wade a moonlit brook.
Birds scatter; just a few are left at all.

(Translated from the Chinese of Li Po)

A. M. JUSTER

Autumn Night

Night air, incessant rustlings—
and dreaming seem to last all year.

Lamps faintly light a shadowed tear;
leaves fall and stir sad songs from strings.

I mark the moments etching space,
a thin monk praying to the wall

as morning bells from somewhere call
and countless feelings leave no trace.

(Translated from the Chinese of Yu T'ung)

Crowded Skies

As a matter of fact, I did notice
a sow followed by a string of piglets
straining to stay airborne
with their unfamiliar wings
as they crossed my line of vision
outside the kitchen window.

Then the doorbell rang,
and I found a crisply dressed
but sumptuous woman at my door.
She announced she was
from the Registry of Motor Vehicles,
apologized for the long lines of the past,
and handed me my new license.
When she asked if there was anything else
she could do for me,
I had a failure of imagination.

Then the phone throbbed.
It was Blue Cross Blue Shield
apologizing for the three years
they spent trying to bill me
for a very expensive hysterectomy
I never had.
They said they had fired the incompetents,
simplified everything,
and my next operation was on them.

When the mail came that afternoon,
there was a sweet-smelling handwritten note
from the cheerleader who rejected
my invitation to the junior prom.

She regretted any distress
her handling of that matter
might have caused me.

I gather air traffic controllers
are up in arms about the crowded skies,
but they will work it out,
I'm sure.

(from the English of Billy Collins)

Bob Dylan's Scandinavian Homesick Blues

Olaf's up in Stockholm slurpin' down the Bourdeaux
I've got a syndrome thinkin' 'bout the styrofoam
The man with the medal, long name, long speech
Says don't be outa reach, cancels me at Long Beach
Look out Swede, there's nothin' I need
Gates knows when but you're textin' me again
You better freak out at Wikileaks makin' up a new trend
The man with the Trump Now! tat in his big den
Wants eleven million five, but you only got ten

Megyn comes, looks great, boss out with no date
Rumors that the press put bugs in his bed but
Phone's tapped (NSA), sources say to run away
They're all in disarray rappin' with the DJ
Look out Pete, don't Facebook or tweet
Plow through the cold snows, don't be no-shows
Better shirk at work from those that carry on with
        Countin' Crows
Strike a vain pose, write urbane prose
You don't need a GPS to know which way the van goes

Ah, old new, old shoes, swill a bit of cheap booze
Slept well, had a snooze, knew judges there were gonna choose
Have fun, go run, go nuts, go brood
Be rude, get sued, call a lawyer if you're screwed
Look out Sven, you got a dry pen
From cheese balls, slackers, old-time sleazeballs
Hangin' round with frackers
Guy with the Balzac lookin' for a new snack
Don't eat the crackers, watch for third-rate actors

Ah, phoned out, zoned out
Be brisk, take risk
Lutefisk, get lost
Get tossed, try so hard to defrost
Get stoned, get real, get pissed
Don't twerk, don't twist
60 years of singin' and they put you on the shortlist
Look out Lars, they'll take you to Mars
Better wolf down the reindeer, find yourself a plain beer
Don't catch Dane fear, you can't survive a train veer
Don't wanna be a hack, you better floss plaque
The lies won't take cuz this pain here makes the brain clear.

(from the English of Bob Dylan)

NOTES ON THE TRANSLATIONS

Saint Aldhelm (ca. 635–640 AD–709) was the "first British man of letters" and arguably wrote the first poem other than a hymn in rhyme and accentual meter. The answers to the riddles are (in order): moon; file; scales; cauldron.

Eucheria was probably the wife of a poet in the literary circle of Venantius Fortunatus (ca 535–ca 605). This poem is her only extant work, and I believe it is the oldest extant humorous poem by a woman in Latin or a Romance language.

A.E. Housman (1859–1936) was a brilliant classical scholar and poet. This love elegy for the unrequited love of his life, Moses Jackson, is the last Latin poem written by a major poet. Due to the poem's then-risky subject matter, Housman buried it in his introduction to his edition of Manilius.

Li Po (701–762) (also referred to as Li Bo and Li Bai) led a tumultuous life (escape from a death sentence for treason, at least four wives) but became one of the greatest and most influential Chinese poets.

The brilliant career of poet, playwright, and spy Christopher Marlowe (1564–1593) was cut short by his murder under mysterious circumstances—not long after he himself was acquitted of murder by the corrupt judge (a relative of Marlowe's by marriage) who is the subject of Marlowe's one extant Latin poem.

Gwerful Mechain (1462–1500) is one of the greatest Welsh poets; many feminist scholars have embraced her verse in recent years. Her *englyn* is the oldest extant poem by a woman objecting to domestic violence.

Oromo is a language (exclusively oral until recently) of about thirty million people in Ethiopia and Kenya. Traditional Oromo proverbs have a strong rhythm and often rhyme.

Rainer Maria Rilke (1875–1926) wrote hundreds of largely overlooked poems in French (and some in Russian) in addition to his famous German poems.

Arthur Rimbaud rocked the Paris literary world as a teenager, but after the end of a violent affair with French poet Paul Verlaine, left France in his early twenties and never (to anyone's knowledge) wrote poetry again.

Yu T'ung (1618–1704) was a prolific Chinese poet and playwright.

ABOUT THE AUTHOR

A. M. Juster is the author of nine previous books of original and translated poetry: *Longing for Laura* (Birch Brook Press, 2001), *The Secret Language of Women* (University of Evansville Press, 2003), *The Satires of Horace* (University of Pennsylvania Press, 2008), *Tibullus' Elegies* (Oxford University Press, 2012), *Saint Aldhelm's Riddles* (University of Toronto Press, 2015), *Sleaze & Slander: Selected Comic Verse 1995–2015* (Measure Press, 2016), *The Billy Collins Experience* (Kelsay Books, 2016), *The Elegies of Maximianus* (University of Pennsylvania Press, 2018), and *John Milton's The Book of Elegies* (Paideia Institute Press 2019). His work has appeared in *Poetry, Paris Review, Hudson Review, Rattle, The New Criterion, Southwest Review, Barrow Street, North American Review,* and many other publications.

Rachel Hadas selected his *The Secret Language of Women* for the 2002 Richard Wilbur Award. He is the only three-time winner of the Howard Nemerov Sonnet Award and is a winner of the Willis Barnstone Translation Prize.

A graduate of Yale and Harvard with two honorary degrees, he lives outside of Boston.